宗教の羅針盤

● ズバリ!! 図式で考える

西川義光 著 〈日英対訳版〉

The Religion Compass
A Graphic Approach to Understanding Religions

Gikō Nishikawa <Bilingual Guide>

まえがき

　世界各地には、いろいろな宗教があります。その中で、世界三大宗教と言われる宗教が、キリスト教・イスラム教・仏教といわれるものです。他にも、膨大な数の宗教が存在しています。伝統的な宗教に加え、新興宗教も数多くあります。宗教それぞれに教学や行動規範が示されており、それらをどのように理解していいのか、困惑するのが当然です。自分と関わりのある宗教を学ぶことはあっても、他の宗教については無関心になってしまいます。

　私は、比較宗教学を研究していた頃、個々の宗教学の解説書を抽出して読みました。そして、宗教間の垣根を越えて理解を深める方法を思惟した上で、宗教教義構造を理解するため、図形による分析に取り組みました。神仏と自己の関係に注目し、それを図式化する方法なら、それぞれの宗教固有の権威や信者の持つ感情等に影響されることなく、冷静に理解が可能になると考えました。たとえば、目前にある建物に対して、実物を見て理解する方法と、その建物の設計図を見て理解するようなものです。本書では大胆に正面から個々の宗教の教学構造を考察・図式化し、その取り組みのシステムを、「宗教の羅針盤」と名付けました。

　私は仏教徒ですが、人類の平和と人々が心の平安をもてる世界の創出に、種々の宗教の本質を理解し、対話の場を設ける取り組みが宗教者にとって必要だと思います。未来に向かって、単に自分の宗教の枠に留まるだけでなく、国・民族・人種・宗教の垣根を越えた「広くて大きな視点」をもつことが必要です。

　現在でも、ユダヤ教・キリスト教・イスラム教の間において対立意識があります。過去には悲惨な歴史があり、対話が難しい状態です。

　異宗教の人たちが、お互いの信仰を理解しあうことを可能とするために、この書ができました。

　近い将来、人類が、国・民族・人種・宗教の垣根を越え、お互いの宗教・思想を認めて理解し、平和創出への願いを共有できるように、宗教

Preface

Christianity, Islam, and Buddhism are generally considered to be the three major world religions. There are many more besides these three, however - some traditional and some new. Because each professes its own religious and ethical concepts, it is only natural that one has difficulty making sense of them. In addition, although a person might study a religion with which he or she feels a personal connection, he or she will probably be indifferent to the others.

When I was a comparative religion student, I read extracts of the theologies of individual religions. I then wondered how to overcome the differences dividing religions so as to facilitate mutual understanding. I finally came up with a way of depicting the structure of religious creeds in graphic form. I thought that, if I focused on the relationship between Divine Power and the Power of Self and expressed it in a schematic manner, without being influenced by each religion's claims of unique authority or its believers' emotions, it would be possible to calmly and objectively analyze religious doctrine. It would be similar to understanding a building by looking at its blueprints rather than by just looking at its exterior. In this book, I tried to come to grips with the doctrinal structures of individual religions by describing them diagrammatically, an approach I have nicknamed a 'religion compass'.

Although I am a Buddhist, I think that in order for the world to become a harmonious place where people can enjoy peace of mind it is necessary for people to understand the essences of various religions. Only in this way will we be able to engage in a mutual dialog. For the sake of the future, it is not enough to understand our own religion; we must also view things from a broad perspective that transcends national, ethnic, racial, and religious boundaries.

Judaism, Christianity, and Islam share a turbulent past marked by mutual antagonism. Even today the relationship between these religions is marked by conflict, and dialog is difficult.

This book was written in the hopes that it would help people of

者が対話の場を設ける役割を担っていくことを期待します。
　なお、本書の英訳にあたっては、ジョン・ベンソン（John Hart Benson）氏にご協力いただきました。深く感謝いたします。

真宗大谷派　専称寺住職
西　川　義　光

専称寺/Senshō-ji Temple

different faiths to better understand one another.

I look forward to a time in the near future when the world will be a harmonious place where people understand and respect the religions of others and are able to transcend national, ethnic, racial, and religious barriers. Hopefully, this book will play a role in making a peaceful world a reality.

Finally, I would like to thank John Hart Benson for his assistance in translating the Japanese text into English.

Gikō Nishikawa

Head Abbot of Senshō-ji Temple,
Ōtsu City, Shiga Prefecture, Japan

目　　次

まえがき 2

序章　宗教の羅針盤 8

第1章　力関係の枠組み 10
　1.「自己」○・「他者」□・「仲介者」△の基本図形　10
　2.「自己力」と「他者力」の力関係の位置付け　12
　　（1）A型＜自己力＞の考察　12
　　（2）B型＜自己力＋他者力＞の考察　12
　　（3）C型＜他者力＞の考察　20
　　（4）D型＜A〜C型に属さないタイプ＞の考察　22

第2章　連続の枠組み 24

第3章　力関係の枠組みと連続関係の枠組みの結合 28
　1.　イエス・キリスト / 釈迦牟尼仏　28
　2.　エラスムス　28
　3.　ル　タ　ー　30
　4.　親　　　鸞　30
　5.　道　　　元　32

第4章　羅針盤をもっての思惟 34
　1.　上座部仏教と大乗仏教　34
　2.　新興宗教　36
　3.　歴史をかえりみて　38
　4.　他者（救済者）との関係　40
　5.　三大宗教の最終目標　42
　6.　人は平等の存在　44
　7.　私自身についての考察　46
　8.　宗教の違いを超えて　50

まとめ 52

参考文献 60

Contents

Preface 3

Introduction 9

Chapter 1: Framework of Power Relation...11

  1. Basic Symbols: Power of Self ◯ , the Other Power ☐ , Intermediary △   11

  2. Framework of Power Relation: Power of Self and the Other Power   13

    (1) Consideration of Type A <Power of Self>   13

    (2) Consideration of Type B   <Power of Self +the Other Power>   13

    (3) Consideration of Type C < the Other Power >   21

    (4) Type D <Exception Not Conforming to Types A - C>   23

Chapter 2: Frameworks of Continuity...25

Chapter 3: Power Relationship Frameworks and Continuity Frameworks in

Combination...29

  1. Jesus Christ / Shakyamuni Buddha   29

  2. Erasmus   29

  3. Luther   31

  4. Shinran   31

  5. Dōgen   33

Chapter 4: Speculations with Compass in Hand...35

  1. Theravada Buddhism and Mahayana Buddhism   35

  2. New Religions   37

  3. A Glance Back at History   39

  4. Relationship with the Other Power (Savior)   41

  5. The Goals of the Big Three Religions   43

  6. People Are Equal   45

  7. A Look at Myself   47

  8. Transcending Religious Differences   51

Summary..53

References..61

序章　宗教の羅針盤

　この書は、ある女性から

「私たちの真理は、キリスト教なら聖書、イスラム教ならコーラン、仏教なら経典を読むことから理解が生まれます。

　しかし、身近な人と宗教が違う場合、何か違和感を覚えます。人生の熟年期を迎えた今、どうか、異宗教の人たちと客観的・合理的に理解しあえる方法を教えて下さい。」

と言われたことが機縁となり、私の過去の研究を回顧しながらわかりやすいように解説しようと思い執筆しました。

　私は、以前に比較宗教学を研究したことがあります。その前に仏教学・真宗学・キリスト教神学を学びました。その後に、英文聖書と仏教漢文経典、異宗教に説かれている教学解説書を横に並べ、各々に説かれる教義構造を図形で理解しようと試みました。各々の宗教の全体像を図形による教学構造で理解できれば、各宗教の持つ独特な見解に迷わされることなく、冷静に自分で、教学に説かれる組織構造の理解が可能になると思惟しました。世界にある様々な宗教を大きな海と比喩し、自分の船が海を航海するためには、自分の現在地と航海目的地を知る道具が必要になります。それが、「宗教の羅針盤」です。自分の宗教を正しく理解し、他宗教との違いが認識できます。当たり前のことですが、実存するものと表記されているものとは違います。ここでは、各宗教の説く教義構築構造を図形で思惟し、真実のあるべき歩みへの理解を深めることを目的とします。この考察にあたり、各宗教の尊称や肩書きは省略します。

Introduction

This book came about because a woman once asked me a question:

'We're taught that for Christians truth is found in the Bible, for Muslims it's found in the Quran, and for Buddhists it's found in the sutras. However, I feel awkward when I'm around believers of different religions. I'm growing old, and I'd like to know if there is some way I can objectively and rationally understand people of other faiths.'

This question caused me to look back at my past research and to try to present it in an easy-to-understand manner.

Before becoming a student of comparative religion, I studied Buddhism, Shin (Pure Land) sect Buddhism, and Christianity. Finally, I placed an English Bible and the Buddhist sutras (written in Chinese characters) side by side. I studied them along with explanations of different religious doctrines and attempted to make diagrams to explain those doctrines' organizational structures. I reasoned that if I could comprehend the structure of a doctrine by means of an overall graphic depiction of the religion then I could analyze a religion without being distracted by its certainty of its own uniqueness. Imagine the various religions of the world as one big ocean across which we are trying to navigate. We need a tool to show us our present location as well as our destination. That tool is what I call a 'religion compass'. Only by correctly understanding our own religion can we recognize how it differs from other religions. In this study, I aim at deepening our understanding of the truth by graphically depicting the structure of each religion's doctrine. In my discussion religious honorifics and titles will be omitted.

第1章　力関係の枠組み

1.「自己」○・「他者」□・「仲介者」△の基本図形

　初めに、「羅針盤」の作成をするために、神仏や人の位置を図形で定義したいと思います。私たち「自己」を○（丸）とし（図1）、対峙する「他者」である神・仏・全知全能者・無限存在等を□（四角）と表記します（図2）。さらに、各宗教教団の代表的存在である法王・教皇・法主・座主・門主等、教団における人でありながら宗教上の教導的立場の存在を、「仲介者」△（三角）と表記します（図3）。

　これより、各宗教上の名称を使わず、「神と人」、「佛と人」等の存在関係を抽象的に図形に置き換えます。

　まずは両者の力関係に着目していきます。人の持つ力を、「自己力」と定義します。その力は「時間・空間における自己の力」と位置付けます。それに対し、人に対して大きな力を有する神仏の存在を「他者力」と定義し、その力を「時間・空間を超越する他者の力」と位置付けます。では、具体的に図式で表記してみましょう。

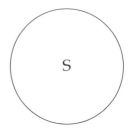

図1　「自己」

図2　「他者」

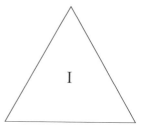

図3　「仲介者」

Chapter 1: Framework of Power Relation

1. Basic Symbols: Power of Self ◯, the Other Power ☐, Intermediary △

In order to make the 'compass', I would first like to define the positions of Man and Divine Power. A circle ◯ represents the Power of Self (**Fig. 1**), our human power or human nature. A square ☐ denotes the Other Power, by which I mean an omniscient and infinite divine being such as God or Buddha (**Fig. 2**). A triangle △ stands for an intermediary figure who is the respresentative or leader of a given religion, for example the Catholic Church's Pope (**Fig. 3**).

I will next describe God/Man and Buddha/Man relationships by means of abstract diagrams that dispense with standard religious terminology.

I will begin by focusing on the power relationships between the two Powers. I define the power of a person as the Power of Self, a finite power in space and time. On the other hand, there is another power, a great natural power that is infinite and beyond space and time. This is the Other Power, the power of God or Buddha. Let's imagine these Powers as geometric shapes.

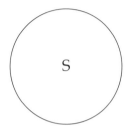

Fig. 1 the Self

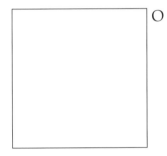

Fig. 2 the Other

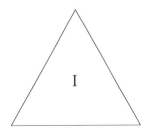

Fig. 3 Intermediary

2.「自己力」と「他者力」の力関係の位置付け

　基本図形が形成できたので、力の働く方向を→(矢印)で表現します。
　すると、「自己」○と「他者」□の力関係の枠組の組み合わせは、おおむね次の三種類に分類されます。

(1) A型＜自己力＞の考察

　キリスト教で説かれている神の子・聖霊・神であるキリストは、人の現罪を贖うために十字架で張りつけにされ、死後復活して神となっているので、「他者」□の存在といえます。

　仏教を説いた釈迦は、修行して煩悩を滅し、仏陀(正覚者)となりました。それは、仏になる力を持つ者のみが、仏になれることを意味し、時空に縛られない「他者」

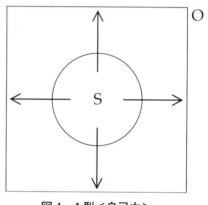

図4　A型＜自己力＞

□の存在といえます。キリストと釈迦は、教義から導くと、神・仏の存在であり、A型となります(図4)。

(2) B型＜自己力＋他者力＞の考察

　ここに、多数の宗教が存在しています。＜自己力＋他者力＞の力関係の宗教では、最終目標への配分比率は無数に考えられますが、理解しやすくするために、三例の相対比率を設定して考察することにします。

2. Framework of Power Relation: Power of Self and the Other Power

Now that the basic shapes and their meanings have been decided, the directions in which power moves can be shown by means of arrows (→).

The possible power relationships between the Self ○ and the Other □ can roughly be classified into the following three types of frameworks.

(1) Consideration of Type A <Power of Self>

Christianity teaches that Christ - the Son of God, the Holy Spirit, God - died on the cross in order to redeem the sins of mankind and was later resurrected. As God, he can be described as being an Other Power □.

Shakyamuni, who preached Buddhism, meditated and subdued his worldly passions to become the Buddha, or the Enlightened One. Only one who possesses the power to become a Buddha can do so, and he can therefore be described as an 'Other Power' □ who exists beyond space and time. Thus, Christ and Shakyamuni can be equated with God and Buddha respectively. This Type A relationship is shown in **Fig. 4**.

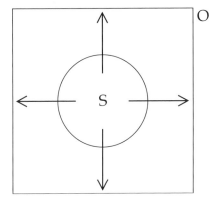

Fig. 4 Type A <Power of Self>

(2) Consideration of Type B   <Power of Self + the Other Power>

There are many religions characterized by a <Power of Self + the Other Power> power relationship. In the quest for the final goal of salvation or release, there are countless ways in which the power ratios can vary. For the sake of simplicity, however, I will set three relative ratios and make certain assumptions.

○と□の力配分比率を全体で100％に仮定すれば、次のような仮定の分類が可能です。

相対比率
例1【○50％：□50％】
例2【○99％：□1％】
例3【○1％：□99％】

例1【○50％：□50％】(図5)

「自己」○と「他者」□の間に、「仲介者」△(法王・宗教指導者・聖職者・教主・台主・門主・門首・尊師・座主・大師等々－各宗教団体において、権威・権力を代表する人)が存在する場合があります。この立場の仲介者に、宗教者としての資質が備わっていない間違った見識を持つ者がいれば、追従する信者や信徒等は、その仲介者の妄語を信じて洗脳されることになり、命と引き替えの行動をおこす

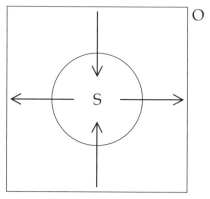

図5　B-1型＜自己力＋他者力＞

ことを求められるような、悲惨な行いへと導かれることがあります。

日本の神風特攻隊員が米国鑑に体当たりで自爆すれば、靖国に生まれて神として祀られました。この場合、条件的に「自己」○50％：「他者」□50％の形と理解できます。死を条件としていることが、宗教にそぐわないと考えます。戦時中の国家権力者が、「仲介者」△の立場に天皇を位置付けていたことが理解できます。

Assuming the power distribution ratio of ○ and □ as 100% as a whole, it is possible to make the following classifications.

Distribution Ratios
Example 1: ○ 50% × □ 50%
Example 2: ○ 99% × □ 1%
Example 3: ○ 1% × □ 99%

Example 1: ○ 50% × □ 50% (Fig. 5)

Between the Power of Self and that of the Other Power, there sometimes stands an Intermediary (a religious organization's representative, such as the Pope, a religious leader, a holy person, a master, etc.) However, if the intermediary does not possess the bona fide qualities and proper insights of a true religious person, he or she can end up misleading or brainwashing his or her followers. This can lead to tragic acts in which lives are sacrificed for the sake of questionable beliefs.

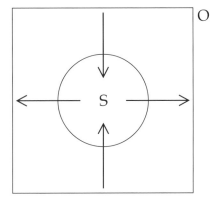

Fig. 5 Type B-1 <Power of Self + the Other Power>

Japanese *kamikaze* pilots, for example, were told that if they blew themselves up, they would become gods and would be enshrined in Yasukuni Shrine. In the case of this power relationship, the Power of Self ○ is 50% and that of the Other Power □ is 50%. I believe, however, that a religion that makes self-sacrifice a condition for salvation/release is not a true one. In the just-cited case of World War II Japan, the Emperor, placed there by the state authorities, occupied the Intermediary △ position.

イスラム教のジハードも同じ形です。信者の自爆で命と引き替えに、祝福されて神の国に生まれると言われます。この場合も、自己犠牲を求められて行動することから、死後に残された家族や友人に痛みを残します。「仲介者」△である宗教的指導者が、自分の意志で自爆するのなら自己責任として理解できなくもありませんが、宗教理解の浅い信者や追随者を死へと導いて、その人達が自爆して死んでいく様子を賞賛しているのは、実に不合理で宗教者としてはとても容認出来るものではありません。

例2【○99％：□1％】(図6)

釈尊を慕う日本の比叡山での千日回峯行者は、悟りへの修行を志します。回峰行で99％を体験し、残りの1％の行は人生をかけて歩むとされています。この場合、明確に自分の位置が確認できるので、人生に迷いが生じないと言えます。修業者には優秀な能力があり、超人的な能力と体力を有していることが考えられ、目標への強い覚悟があることが伺えます。

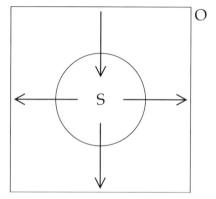

図6　B-2型＜自己力＋他者力＞

例3【○1％：□99％】(図7、図8)

キリスト教カソリックを見てみます。ローマ教会では、法王が存在します。16世紀の人文学者エラスムスは、神の救済に対して、人の「自由意志」を認めているので、B型の＜他者力＋自己力＞と表記できます。神の存在の大きさを説いてますが、人には救済を受け入れる意思の力を認

Islamic jihad shows the same power relationship framework. Jihadists are told that if they sacrifice their lives they will be reborn in Paradise. However, death by self-sacrifice leaves family members and friends in pain. If the Intermediary △ - the religious leader - were to blow himself up, it could perhaps be viewed as a responsible act. But convincing believers who do not possess a deep understanding of their religion to sacrifice themselves and then praising those acts of self-destruction is not only unreasonable but unacceptable.

Example 2: ○ 99% × □ 1% (**Fig. 6**)

Kyoto's Mt. Hiei is the site of a famous Buddhist monastery. In their quest for enlightenment, some of the monastery's monks circumnavigate the top of the mountain a thousand times. Just performing the feat accounts for 99% of their spiritual awakening, while the remaining 1% is said to accumulate from having offered up their lives in the attempt to complete the walk. In this case the large role played by the Self is quite

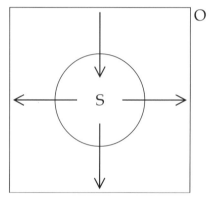

Fig. 6 Type B-2 <Power of Self + the Other Power>

evident, for those who choose to undergo this spiritual training are full of conviction. This thousand-day circuit requires outstanding spiritual ability and almost superhuman physical prowess. Its practitioners obviously possess a strong determination to reach their goal.

Example 3: ○ 1% × □ 99% (**Fig. 7, 8**)

Let's consider Catholicism, a religion headed by a figure called the Pope. The 16th century humanist, Erasmus, asserted that free will plays a part in salvation. Therefore, the Type B framework, < the Other Power + Power of Self>, applies. In Erasmus' thinking, the role played by God in

めているので、この場合B型の中でも【○1％：□99％】と言えます。

　B型を考察して思うのは、「仲介者」△の存在です。彼らが「神の声を聞いた」「真理を悟った」「特別な力を授かった」「霊能力を得た」「宇宙と交信した」「特別な利益を得ることができる」等々を言っている場合は、宗教の本質とは大きく離れることになります。

　このB型で、問題が起こりやすい原因と考えられるのは、「自分には甘く、他人には厳しい人」の特性があります。仮に自分に80％の力を持ちながら、10％しか努力せずに、他の90％の力を求める場合等が考えられます。努力せず多くの結果を願う場合、もはや宗教的思考でなく、自己の欲望充足の為の低俗な行為になってしまいます。

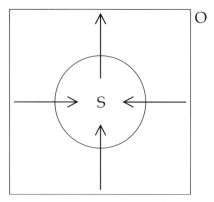

図7　B-3-1型＜自己力＋他者力＞

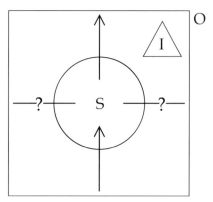

図8　B-3-2型＜自己力＋他者力＞
　　　問題となる型

salvation is the greater one, but man's desire to be saved also plays a part. Among Type B examples, it is one in which the Power of Self ○ has a 1% role in effecting salvation, while the Other Power □ has a 99% role.

Considering Type B diagrams, I cannot help but think about the role of the Intermediary △. When an Intermediary makes such pompous claims as 'I've heard the voice of God', 'I've received the Truth', 'I've received special powers', 'I've become endowed with spiritual power', 'I communicated with Outer Space', or 'I've been granted something wonderful', it seems to me that he or she has strayed from the religion's true essence.

In the case of Type B power relationship frameworks, problems are also likely to occur due to the propensity of individuals to be easy on themselves but hard on others. Someone might exert only a small percent of his or her total potential power, while desiring the Other Power to supply the deficit. Expecting results without being willing to make effort is not a genuinely religious way of thinking and can lead to a kind of behavior that is self-satisfied and vulgar.

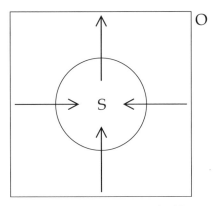

Fig. 7 Type B-3-1 <Power of Self + the Other Power>

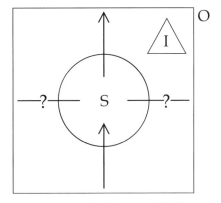

Fig. 8 Type B-3-2 <Power of Self + the Other Power>

(3) C型＜他者力＞の考察(図9)

　13世紀の日本仏教の親鸞は、明恵上人の菩提心のあり方についての批判に対し、阿弥陀如来の他力廻向の念仏を頂き、浄土往生をする絶対他力の教えを説きました。両者に通じるのは、自己力は０％で、無力であり、他者の力を受け入れる他者力の教義構造です。

　16世紀のドイツの宗教改革者ルターは、神の絶対的な恩恵を説いています。ルターは、神の救済における人の「自由意志」を否定し、ひたすら神の救いのみを説きました。正に他者力の教学構造です。

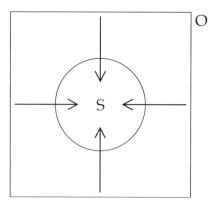

図9　C型＜他者力＞

　この２人に共通するのは、他力の教義を持ち、「仲介者」△の存在が無いことです。そして、天国・極楽(浄土)への救済の起因を、神仏から発したのであるから、自己力の存在が認められません。絶対他者と人との「直接契約、直接約束」であることからして、人は平等であると説かれています。

(3) Consideration of Type C < of the Other Power > (Fig. 9)

In the 13th century, Shinran, in response to criticism from Kegon-sect priest, Myo-e, asserted that merely reciting the *nenbutsu* (a prayer invoking Amida Buddha's name) would enable one to be reborn in the Pure Land. In this doctrinal construct human power is of no account. Power of Self is 0% effective in the quest for salvation/release, which comes about entirely through the offices of the Other Power.

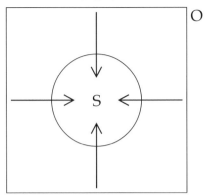

Fig. 9 Type C < Power of Self + the Other Power >

Luther, the 16th century leader of the Protestant Reformation, preached the absolute power of God's grace. He denied that free will played any role in salvation; rather, one's salvation was in the hands of God alone. His teaching fits the 'Other Power's power is absolute' conceptual framework.

Both Shinran and Luther share a belief in the absolute efficacy of the Other Power, and their teachings assign no role to an Intermediary. Whether the goal is Heaven or the Pure Land, salvation/release comes about through the direct offices of God or Buddha, not through any exercise of free will. Each individual has a covenant with and direct access to the Other Power, and in this respect all humans are equal.

(4) D型＜A～C型に属さないタイプ＞の考察(図10)

　仏教の道元は、「正法眼蔵」で、「止観只坐」を説いています。彼は「禅は、仏行そのもの」であると述べています。その場合、自己力と他者力の関係は融合した状態になるので、矢印では表現できません。座禅の行中は仏と一体です。しかし、禅行を解けば煩悩を有するので人の存在です。このように溶けあった「自己」と〇「他者」□の教義構造を図形で表現すると、人の状態を点線で表現できます。

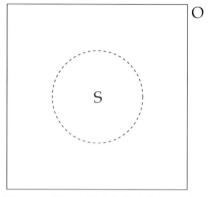

図10　D型＜自己力と他者力の区別がない＞

(4) Type D <Exception Not Conforming to Types A - C> (Fig. 10)

In his collection of essays, *Shōbōgenzō*, the Japanese Zen monk, Dōgen, teaches about *shikantaza*, or mediation without a koan (also called 'selfless meditation'.) He states that when practicing *zazen* (seated meditation) one is in a state of Buddhahood. During *zazen*, the Power of Self and the Other Power merge. Thus, arrows cannot be used to indicate the directions in which power flows. Although the practitioner and the Buddha become one entity during *zazen*, the practitioner reverts to being a human with the usual worldly desires when meditation ends. When this merging of the Power of Self ○ and the Other Power □ is expressed in graphic form, the human power sphere is delineated by means of a dotted line.

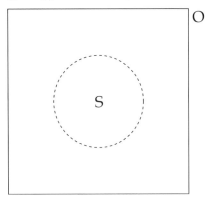

Fig. 10 Type D <No Distinction between Power of Self and the Other Power >

第2章　連続の枠組み

　私たちは、第1章で、力関係の枠組みを、「自己」○と「他者」□の力関係に焦点をあてて考察しました。第2章では、「自己」○と「他者」□の存在関係について考察することにします。

　連続の枠組みを3つの型で表します。

　旧約聖書の源流を共有しているユダヤ教・キリスト教・イスラム教の教義構造は、一神教です。しかも、神は創造主で絶対的存在であり、人とは異質の存在に位置するので、型2に属します(図12)。

　仏教では、煩悩を有する「自己」○と、煩悩のない「他者」□は非連続であるが、「自己」○には仏性を認めているので、煩悩を無くして涅槃(ねはん)の境地に至る事が可能と説いている事から、型3に属する事が出来ます(図13)。

　キリストと釈迦は、□の存在に位置するから、型1の連続(同質)に属すると言えます(図11)。

　興味深いのは、第1章の力関係の枠組みでは、親鸞とルターは同じC型に属していましたが、第2章の連続の枠組みでは別の型になったことです。

　結論を要約すると、キリストと釈迦は型1に属します。キリスト教のエラスムスとルターは、型2に属します。仏教の

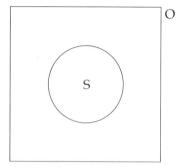

図11　型1　○と□は、連続(同質)

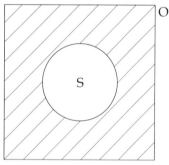

図12　型2　○と□は、非連続(異質)

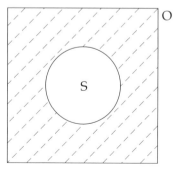

図13　型3　○と□は、連続と非連続(同質＆異質)

Chapter 2: Frameworks of Continuity

In Chapter 1 we considered Power Relation Frameworks focusing on the power relationships between the Power of Self ○ and the Other Power □. In Chapter 2 we will consider the way in which these relationships are continuous, noncontinuous, or both.

I will describe these Frameworks of Continuity by means of three diagrams.

Because Christianity, Judaism, and Islam all share a belief in certain teachings of the Old Testament, they also demonstrate the same basic doctrinal structure. Namely, they are all monotheisms featuring a Divine Creator whose nature is totally unlike that of humans. This is shown in Type 2 (**Fig. 12**).

In Buddhism ○ and □ are essentially heterogeneous, because the former is possessed of worldly passions while the latter is not. However, ○ is capable of desiring Buddha-nature and is thus also capable of subduing worldly passions and entering nirvana. Type 3 illustrates this simultaneously continuous and noncontinuous relationship (**Fig. 13**).

Christ and Shakyamuni are synonymous with □, so ○ and □ exist in homogeneous continuity, as illustrated by Type 1 (**Fig. 11**).

It is interesting to note that in Chapter 1

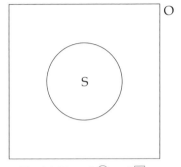

Fig. 11 Type 1 ○ and □, continuous (homogeneous)

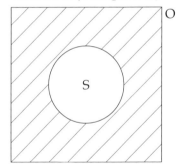

Fig. 12 Type 2 ○ and □, noncontinuous (heterogeneous)

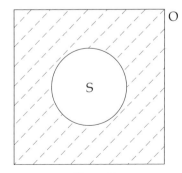

Fig. 13 Type 3 ○ and □, continuous and noncontinuous (homogeneous and heterogeneous)

親鸞と道元は、煩悩を有する人が、到達目標の悟りへと融合するので、型3に属することになります。

both Shinran and Luther fit into the Type C power relationship framework. However, in the Frameworks of Continuity scheme of things, different frameworks apply.

To summarize, Christ and Shakyamuni belong to Type 1, while Erasmus and Luther conform to Type 2. Shinran and Dōgen, however, believe that humans can subdue their worldly passions and achieve enlightenment, a viewpoint illustrated by Type 3.

第3章　力関係の枠組みと連続関係の枠組みの結合

1. イエス・キリスト / 釈迦牟尼仏

この２つの教義は、キリストが神であり、ゴータマ・シッダルタが仏陀であるので、存在が同質であり、常に連続であり、絶対存在です（図14）。

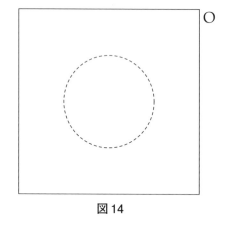

図14

2. エラスムス

カソリックには法王が存在しています。神と人は異質関係であり、エラスムスは人の「自由意志」を認めています。教義構造の図形は、ムハンマド・イブンが神の予言者の地位にあることから、イスラム教の教学構造にもあてはまります（図15）。

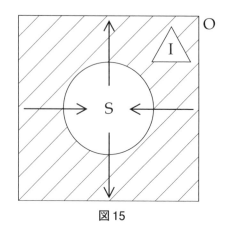

図15

Chapter 3: Power Relationship Frameworks and Continuity Frameworks in Combination

1. Jesus Christ / Shakyamuni Buddha

In Christianity Christ is also God. In Buddhism Gautama Siddharta is also Buddha. They are absolute beings in a homogeneous, continuous relationship (**Fig. 14**).

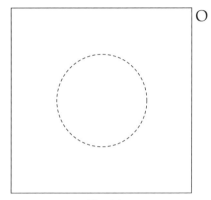

Fig. 14

2. Erasmus

The Catholic Church has an Intermediary, the Pope. God and Man exist in a heterogeneous relationship, but Erasmus recognizes that Man has free will. In a similar manner, Islam's doctrinal structure grants Muhammad Ibn the role of Prophet, an Intermediary. As such, the doctrine of Islam fits the relationships depicted in **Fig. 15**.

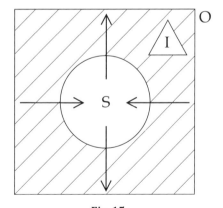

Fig. 15

3. ルター

　創造主の神と人は、全く異質であり、神の一方的な力のみが働きます。人は救済においては無力であるので、絶対他力の形となります(図16)。

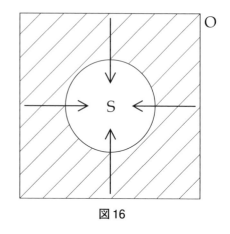

図16

4. 親　鸞

　ルターと同じ絶対他力の形ですが、仏と人の関係は、キリスト教とは異なっています。人に煩悩がある時は非連続関係であり、煩悩が無くなれば仏陀と連続関係の存在となります。ここで、ルターと親鸞の教学上の共通点と相違点が理解できます(図17)。

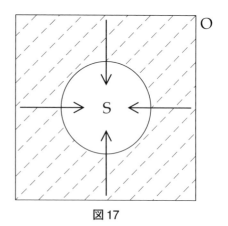

図17

3. Luther

God the Creator and Man are completely heterogeneous in nature. **Fig. 16** illustrates the Other Power's absolute power. Man has no means of effecting his salvation. In that regard, God's power alone is operative, and it moves in one direction.

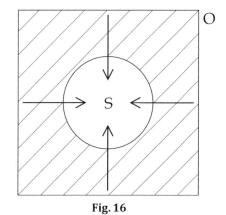

Fig. 16

4. Shinran

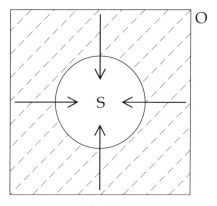

Fig. 17 shows the same absolute Other Power as we saw in the case of Luther. However, the relationship of Buddha and Man is different from the one seen in Christianity between God and Man. When Man is filled with worldly passions, his relationship with Buddha is noncontinuous. When those passions are conquered, however, it changes into a continuous one. Here, the similarities, as well as the differences, between Luther and Shinran can be understood.

Fig. 17

5. 道　元

宗教界において、ユニークな存在です。人が煩悩を有する存在であっても、仏行の禅は、涅槃に通じていると説かれます。禅行が仏行であるから、仏の直接の行なので融和状態であり、矢力の方向は不要となります(図18)。

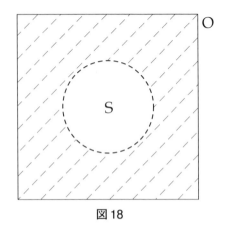

図 18

　表記した宗教者の思想を考究した結合図面を見て、各宗教の絶対他者(神仏)の存在の構成図形が異なり、キリスト教のエラスムスとルターの違いが明らかになりました。仏教の親鸞と道元も異なる結論になりました。このシステムを用いて宗教を理解すれば、自分のいる位置が明らかになり、あり方も思案できます。なお、ここで使用した図形による考察法は、私がアメリカ・ドルー大学で書いた論文 'Power of Self and the Other Power in Christianity and Buddhism.' で発表したものです。

5. Dōgen

Dōgen's place in the realm of religious thought is a unique one. His teaching holds that although human beings are possessed by worldly passions they can reach nirvana when they practice *zazen*. To Dōgen, one attains Buddha-nature when engaged in *zen* meditation. Because ○ and □ exist in a state of compatibility, there is no need for directional arrows in the diagram (**Fig. 18**).

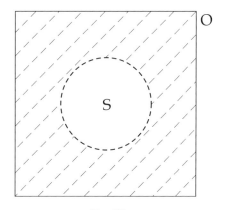

Fig. 18

We have described the teachings of different religious figures in graphic form and then studied various combinations of these frameworks. As a result, we were able to see how concepts concerning absolute beings (God, Buddha) differ from religion to religion. We observed the ways in which the ideas of Erasmus and Luther differ. The differences between Shinran and Dōgen also became apparent. I hope that this method of looking at religions will guide you on your way and aid you as you ponder the best way to live. In constructing the diagrams used here, I have referred to my graduate thesis, 'Power of Self and the Other Power in Christianity and Buddhism.'

第4章　羅針盤をもっての思惟

第1章から第3章の「宗教の羅針盤」はいかがでしたか。宗教といっても、国・地域・時代・文化・民族等によっても、様々な形態があります。各々の宗教に歴史があり、それらの宗教間の優劣を論ずることは、ここでは目的と考えていません。しかし、宗教の本質とは異なると感じる事柄については、私見を述べたいと思います。

1. 上座部仏教と大乗仏教

インドの宗教に、ヒンズー教・ジャイナ教があります。破壊と創造の神々が存在し、人は輪廻すると説いています。その社会環境の中から、仏教が生まれました。仏陀は、煩悩から生じる苦悩の解脱を説きました。さらにカースト制度の社会制度・現実生活から生じる苦悩等からの解脱を説き、涅槃寂静の境地を目標としました。釈迦は弟子に対し、煩悩を滅していく修行法を具体的に示しました。その流れを受けているのが、上座部(小乗)仏教で、釈尊の教えを忠実に実践して悟りを目指しています。仏陀(ゴータマ・シッダルタ)は、涅槃の境地に達するための「三宝印」(諸行無常・諸法無我・涅槃寂静)と「四諦・八正道」の教義を説き、五戒の戒律を説きました。そして、自分が到達した「涅槃」境地へ信者を導こうとしました。それとは別に、釈迦滅後、大乗(大衆部)仏教が生まれました。民衆に目を向けた大乗仏教は、仏と菩薩に出会って悟りを目指す教義なので、さまざまな時代や場所において、新しい教学を展開しました。特にインドの龍樹の空観「色即是空」、天親の唯識「意識はどこからくるのか」の2思想からは、私たちの存在を深く見つめることの大切さが伝わってきます。

日本仏教の親鸞は、「教行信証」において彼が自力から他力へ転入した体験を「三願転入」で説明しています。さらに自力の菩提心(仏になろう

Chapter 4: Speculations with Compass in Hand

Chapters 1 to 3 introduced my notion of a 'religion compass'. I hope you found it interesting. Religions display great variety and come in many forms depending on such variables as nationality, geographical region, culture, and ethnicity. Every religion has its own history. My intent here is not to debate the merits or demerits of individual religions. However, I feel that there are times when people lose sight of a religion's essence, and I would like to express an opinion about this.

1. Theravada Buddhism and Mahayana Buddhism

Hinduism and Jainism are two Indian religions. They teach that there are deities that both create and destroy and that people are reincarnated. In such a context Buddhism was born. Buddha taught that people could be released from the cycle of suffering caused by their worldly passions. He also preached that the sufferings caused by such social structures as the caste system and by those that arise in our everyday lives could be eliminated. The final goal offered by Buddhism was a quiet, still state called nirvana. For his disciples Shakyamuni (Buddha) concretely outlined the spiritual training regimen that they would need to follow in order to subdue their worldly passions and attain nirvana. Theravada Buddhism closely adheres to this regimen, and its followers strive to achieve enlightenment by faithfully practicing Buddha's teaching. To help people achieve nirvana, Buddha taught the Three Treasures Seal - all things change, all things lack inherent identity, nirvana is perfect tranquility - the Noble Four Truths and the Noble Eight-Fold Path, and the Five Precepts. Buddha wanted to lead his disciples to nirvana, a state that he himself had attained. Mahayana Buddhism appeared after the Buddha had died. Appealing to the masses, it stressed enlightenment through the offices of Bosatsu (Bodhisattvas). New doctrines developed at various times and in various places. Two Indian philosophers, Nagarjuna and Vasubandhu, especially influenced the development of Mahayana Buddhism. Nagarjuna wrote that existence

とする心)と絶対他力の菩提心の違いを明確にしました。これは、キリスト教のエラスムスとルターの間で論じられた「自由意志」の論争と呼応する内容であることを指摘しておきます。

　第1章から第3章では、それぞれの宗教が説かれている教学構造を明らかにし、それらを比較しながら考察しました。導かれた判断は、読者に委ねます。しかし、「悪魔の導き・ささやき」が聞こえてくるようなものについては、理解を深めるための意見を述べさせて頂きます。

2. 新興宗教

　まず、日本の、オウム真理教の殺害事件、イスラム教のジハード(殉職死者)、戦時中の日本の神風特攻隊等の方々の思考構造を、図14の図式に乗せて、客観的に理解して頂きたいと思います。

　少し新興宗教にも触れたいと思います。団体Sでは、教祖と言われる人物を「本仏」といっています。仏教経典では、弥勒菩薩が56億7千万年後に仏になり、衆生を救うと仏教典に記されてあります。政治的関心の高いことからして、仏教を都合よく利用したいと考えていると感じます。オウム真理教の教祖にも同じように感じます。大乗教典を解読しないで、都合のいい教えを展開するのは、私には問題外です。

　K教団では、悟りを得た仏陀の教えを、全宇宙に伝えるべき真実の法であると述べています。人間は神の子・仏の子であることを自覚した上で他者へ愛を与え、真理を探求し、自分の心を見つめ直し、社会全体を向上させる心構えをもつという現世での「魂修行」を説いています。現代の四正道として「愛・知・反省・発展」を提唱しています。現代風に仏教学をアレンジしたものと思いますが、私には、宗教に対峙した時にある篤い求道心が感じられず、昔からいわれる、「仏陀とダイバダッダは

is changeableness, while Vasubandhu expounded on the composition of consciousness.

In his treatise *Kyōgyōshinshō*, the Japanese Buddhist, Shinran, explains how his study of *sanganten'nyū* ('three-prayers-turning-in') brought about his shift from reliance on *jiriki*, or self power, as a means of attaining liberation to *tariki*, or other power (ie., Amida Buddha). He also clarifies the difference between the desire to attain Buddha-nature by means of self power and attaining it through the other power of Amida Buddha. Interestingly, this corresponds to the debate between Erasmus and Luther regarding free will.

In Chapters 1 to 3, I clarified the structures of the teachings of various religions and compared them. I will leave it to my readers to make their own judgments. However, I would like to offer my opinions about some things that I think are dubious or misleading. I hope it will aid in understanding.

2. New Religions

First of all, I would like to consider the conceptual frameworks underlying such phenomena as Japan's Aum Shinrikyo and its sarin gas attack on the Tokyo subway, Islamic jihad, and the *kamikaze* pilot attacks of World War II. I would like to look at them objectively in light of the power relationship framework shown in Fig. 14.

I would also like to briefly touch on the subject of new religions. For example, a certain religious organization that I will call 'S' refers to its leader as a 'Genuine Buddha'. According to Buddhist sutras, however, the Miroku Bosatsu (the Buddha of the Future) will become a Buddha in 5.67 billion years. The sutras say that he will save the masses. Given the keen interest in politics displayed by 'S', it seems to me that it is conveniently using Buddhism for its own ends. I feel the same way about Aum Shinrikyo, and I think it is out of the question for such groups to develop such new, self-serving teachings without first undertaking a thorough study of the Mahayana scriptures.

Another new religious organization, 'K', says that the teachings of the enlightened Buddha should be relayed to the entire universe as the 'True Law'. It says that human beings are 'Children of God and Buddha' and

紙一重」ということを思い出します。その他数多くの宗教がありますが、注目される事については今後も取り組んでいきます。

3. 歴史をかえりみて

　歴史をかえりみると、社会権力者が自分の信じる宗教を正当化して、他の宗教者を迫害している事実があります。キリスト教徒が侵略者と共に、先住民の宗教文化を破壊したり、イスラム教徒を迫害したり、イスラム教徒がキリスト教徒に反撃したりしています。イスラム教では、「偶像崇拝」を否定しているので、仏教遺跡を公然と破壊したことがあります。

　仏教徒が仏像をつくったのには理由があります。元来は、法輪や仏足跡が礼拝の対象でした。しかし、ガンダーラ地方に住んでいた仏教徒は、漢民族に家や土地を奪われ、山岳地へと逃げました。彼らはヨーロッパから伝わった彫刻技術を身に付けていたので、伝わっている仏陀伝記を彫刻し、心から慕っている仏陀の姿に思いをはせて仏像を創作したので、それらが身近な信仰の対象になったのです。仏教では、仏像や菩薩像を大切にして、仏像の前に立つことは、仏を身近に感じる方便（真実に導く）として理解し、その上で、仏と自分との連帯を感じるものとして理解されるからです。

　イスラム教徒が十字架を壊したのを見た牧師が、コーランを焼却したというニュースを見ましたが、イスラム教徒が怒りの声を上げていたのが印象的でした。歴史的構造物や宗教的貴重物の破損だけでなく、他宗教者と命のやり取りをするなど、宗教観の違いから紛争が生じる問題もあります。

　宗教の社会的役割を考えれば、破壊を目的にした行動を起こす前に、感情に流されず、知恵・理性に基づいた合理的な判断が必要です。人は、

preaches that people should love one another, seek the truth, engage in self-reflection, and do good things for the improvement of society as a whole. They advocate a version of the Noble Four Truths that stresses the virtues of love, knowledge, self-reflection, and self-improvement. This strikes me as being a modern take on Buddhist doctrine, but I think it is a misguided approach. I am reminded of the saying about Buddha and Devadatta: they might appear to be the same, but in reality they are completely different.

3. A Glance Back at History

Looking back in history, we see that those in positions of power always tried to make their religion the main one. They oppressed believers of other religions. Christians, for example, joined forces with invaders who destroyed the religious cultures of the original inhabitants. Christians persecuted Muslims, who then fought back against Christians. Islam rejects iconography, and for that reason Muslims publicly carried out the destruction of a famous Buddhist ruin.

Buddhist believers began making Buddhist images for a reason. In the beginning the Wheel (of Buddha's Law) and the Buddha's footprint were the only objects of worship. However, that changed when Han Chinese attacked Buddhists living in the Gandhara region. Robbed of their homes and land, the Buddhists fled to mountainous areas. They had learned the techniques of sculpture from the West, and in their new home they began sculpting scenes from the Buddha's life. Imagining the form of their beloved Buddha, they also made images that became objects of devotion. To Buddhists, images of the Buddha and the Bodhisattvas are held in great esteem. They enable the worshipper to feel close to the Buddha and find a comforting sensation of solidarity with him.

I saw on the news that a pastor who had seen Muslims destroy a cross retaliated by burning a Quran. The angry reaction of Muslims was quite something to behold. Because of religious differences, not only valuable historical structures and religious objects are destroyed, but fights break out and lives are lost as well.

Considering the role played by religion in society, it seems to me that before acting in a such a destructive manner, we should make rational

自分には甘く他人には厳しい判断をします。他の思想を持った方への思いやりが大切です。

4. 他者（救済者）との関係

　ここからは、さらに人と「他者」（救済者）□との関係を考察していきます。まず問題となるのは、人と「他者」□を成立させている「現在の世界の存在」との関係です。

　キリスト教・イスラム教・ユダヤ教の教義構造は、一神教となっています。しかも、神は絶対的存在であり、人とは明らかに異質で最上存在として位置しています。

　宗教の本質を理解するために、図式で理解を深めていけば、各々の宗教教義構造の長所と短所が理解できます。今回の考察で、力関係の枠組みのＢ型（自己力＋他己力）において、人的要素が加わる宗教では、本来宗教の持つ幸福追求とは違う、政治力を有する権力者に利用される問題がある事を危惧します。「仲介者」△の存在がある場合は、その立つ位置を分析して理解を深めると、「仲介者」△の役割が理解できます。

　教祖「イエス・キリスト」は、神への絶対的な信仰と隣人愛を説きました。唯一絶対神には、「創造主」「神の子」「精霊」が含まれます。罪（原罪・行いの罪・思いの罪）を救うためにキリストがこの世に現れ、教えを説いたとされています。「神・神の子・聖霊」の三位一体教義から、神の子キリストは神として位置付けられています。「山上の垂訓」の教義、「七つのサクラメント」の戒律が説かれ、大きくはローマカソリック（旧教）とプロテスタント（新教）に分類されます。

　イスラム教の神「アッラー」は全知全能であり、万物の創造主です。教義の基礎に旧約聖書を用いているのは、キリスト教徒と同じです。教祖「ムハンマド・イブン＝アブドウッラーフ」は、ラマダーンの月のある日、天使ジブリールの啓示を受けました。神の声を聞き、それを人々に伝える預言者として活動しました。イスラム教では、マハメッドは預言者であり、最上の仲介者に位置しているのがキリスト教と異なります。

judgments based on knowledge rather than allow our emotions to get the better of us. As individuals, however, we tend to be easy on ourselves, but hard on others. Therefore, it is all the more important to treat people of other faiths with consideration.

4. Relationship with the Other Power (Savior)

Let's once again consider the relationship between humans and the Other Power (Savior) □ . The first problem that arises is the existence of the modern world and the way in which it affects our relationship with the Other Power.

Christianity, Islam, and Judaism are all monotheistic religions. Moreover, their gods are absolute beings of a very different nature from that of humans. They are divine.

In order to understand a religion's essence, it is important to deeply understand its structure. Only then can we understand its good and bad points. In the present discussion the Type B power framework (Power of Self + the Other Power) is relevant. In religions that have a structure involving a human leader or representative, there is always a danger that that person will wield power to suit his or her own ends, rather than for the benefit of all. Recognizing that such an Intermediary △exits, however, means that figure's position can be analyzed and his or her role understood.

Jesus Christ taught that people should believe absolutely in God and love their neighbor. There is one and only one God, who embodies the Creator, the Son of God, and the Holy Spirit. Christ appeared on Earth in order to redeem our sins (original, of deed, and of thought). The doctrine of the Trinity (Father, Son, Holy Ghost) places Christ, the Son of God, as God. The doctrine of the Sermon on the Mount and the Seven Sacraments were taught. Christianity separated into Roman Catholicism and Protestantism.

Allah, the God of Islam, is omniscient, omnipotent, and the creator of all things. Both Islam and Christianity share a belief in the Old Testament. One day in the month of Ramadan, Muhammad Ibn received a sign from the angel Gabriel. After hearing the voice of God, he became a prophet, preaching to the people. In Islam he is regarded as a prophet, and, thus, in the structure of Islam, he has the role of top Intermediary. In this regard, his position is different from that of Christ in Christianity.

アッラーは、性別・民族・国籍・社会的地位に関係なく、慈愛と慈悲を与えますが、この世を終わらせることができる神でもあります。「コーラン」では、イスラム教徒に、神・天使・預言者・啓典・来世・天命の六信に信仰をささげることを説いています。この「六信」教義と「五行」の戒律が説かれ、シーア派とスンニー派に分類されます。

　宗教教団といっても、政治と密着している宗教団体や、政治と距離を置こうとする宗教団体等さまざまです。宗教者の持つ教義内容を冷静に理解しやすくするために、図式化をしました。ここでは、その宗教の教義の優劣等を論じるのを目的とせず、その宗教者の説く教義構造に基づき、人と向かい合う対象者との力関係を分析し、どのような関係構造なのかを、「力関係の枠組み」(Frame Works of Power Relations)で分析し、図面上で位置づけ、特に世界三大宗教と言われるキリスト教・イスラム教・仏教を意識しながら、考察を進めました。この本の引用文献資料等については、私のアメリカ留学時代に執筆した論文'Power of Self and the Other Power in Christianity and Buddhism.'(Gikō Nishikawa, Drew University, USA, 1980)にあるので、そちらで確認して下さい。

5. 三大宗教の最終目標

　三大宗教に説かれる最終目標は、「神の国・天国、極楽・浄土、悟り、涅槃等」へ到達することです。宗教の中には、人の欲望を満足させるようなことを言う場合もあります。私には、自分にとって都合の良い場所だけを得ようとしているとしか思えません。人が宗教から得られると思うものに、「幸福感・達成感・充実感・満足感・静寂感・安心感」等があります。宗教の教義内容を理性的に分析して理解せず、安易に最終目標に近づくことを願う人が多すぎると思います。

　世界で多くの人に影響を及ぼしている宗教に、エルサレムを聖地としているユダヤ教・キリスト教・イスラム教があります。各々神の名称は異なりますが、三宗教の教学構造は同型の一神教といえます。勿論、教学用語は違いますが、唯一神の存在、神の国に生まれようとする目標到

Allah shows compassion and mercy regardless of gender, race, nationality, and social status. He also has the power to bring the world to an end. The Quran says that Muslims must subscribe to six fundamental beliefs, or Six Articles of Faith. A Muslim must believe in: 1) one God (Allah), 2) the angels of God, 3) the Quran, 4) the prophet (Muhammad), 5) the Day of Judgment, 6) the supremacy of God's will. In addition to the Six Articles, there are five precepts called the Five Pillars of Islam. Islam is split into two main sects, Shia and Sunni.

There are many types of religious organizations. Some, for example, get involved in politics, while others keep a distance. In order to make sense of these various, often confusing, religions and their doctrines, I resorted to using schematic diagrams. In this discussion I do not intend to pass judgment on the worth of those doctrines. By putting the teachings of religious figures into the form of conceptual frameworks, I wanted to understand power relationships. By means of these Power Relation Frameworks, I analyzed the three main religions of Christianity, Islam, and Buddhism. In this paper I have drawn on various sources. These are cited in the thesis that I wrote when I was an exchange student in a U.S. graduate school. Please refer to 'Power of Self and the Other Power in Christianity and Buddhism.'(Gikō Nishikawa, Drew University. USA, 1980).

5. The Goals of the Big Three Religions

The Kingdom of God, Heaven, Paradise, the Pure Land, enlightenment, and nirvana: reaching these places or states of being are the stated goals of the world's three main religions. However, some religions seem to be only offering their believers a way of satisfying personal desires. Indeed, it seems to me that some people only want to take from religion what suits their needs. Some of the things that people hope to gain from religion are a sense of happiness, achievement, satisfaction, tranquility, and safety. Many people fail to clearly analyze and comprehend religious doctrine. Instead, they seem to be just hoping to find an easy access to the final goal.

Judaism, Christianity, and Islam - religions with a great number of followers - all consider Jerusalem to be a holy place. Although the names of their respective gods differ, they all share the same basic structure: they are

達点が明確です。「与えられた人生は一度きり」の教義は、人には理解しやすい構造となっています。これに比べ、多神教の教義は複雑な人格的要素が加わっているので、難解になります。

マハメッドからいえば、先出のキリストは預言者と認めていますが、自らの優秀さを宣言した上で、コーランを正当な拠り所と教えました。世界三大宗教といわれるイスラム教は、政治経済との関連性が強く、仏教は、釈迦が世界とのしがらみを持とうとしなかったのでそれが薄く、明らかにキリスト教とイスラム教は、仏教の教義構造からくる社会との関わり方は異なります。

6. 人は平等の存在

宗教で必ず問題となるのが、人種・人権問題です。権威・権力を好む人には、自分より人を下に位置づけようと考えます。現在に至る人類の歴史を理解していれば、このような愚かなことを考えません。私の属する真宗大谷派の代表、宗教総長に対して、「人権を大切にし、差別を起こさせない、教団の共通認識の構築」を申し出ましたが、無関心なのか、いい加減な回答しかありませんでした。絶対他力の教えの礎にする教団なら、現在を生きる人、社会に対して、その教団の明確な教団としての意思表示があるべきです。「ルターと親鸞」は、それぞれの教学に明確な生き方を示しています。彼らのような宗教指導者をもち、明確な教えを説く場合、明確に社会貢献に対する取組みをしていないのは、その教団の愚かさであり怠慢です。キリスト教の中には、差別解消への取組みを実行している教団があります。大乗仏教においては、人種差別・人権意識が乏しいことがよく見受けられます。教団内において、差別・偏見をなくすための共通認識を持とうとしないのは、責任者の自覚の欠如からです。特に絶対他力救済の教義を説いた親鸞とルターには、無知な亡者の集まりと映るでしょう。彼らは、人間の傲慢さを認めない生き方を求めるからです。つまり、宗教者としての在り方に問題があると指摘して

all monotheistic religions. Of course, their terminology differs, but they all posit the existence of one God, and the clear goal of each is rebirth in the Kingdom of God. Such doctrines that maintain that life is a one-time-only affair are relatively easy to understand. In comparison, polytheistic religions that have a confusing number of deities and divinities are more difficult to comprehend.

Muhammad recognized his predecessor Christ as a prophet, but he proclaimed himself to be superior and said that the Quran was the legitimate word of God. Of the Big Three religions, Islam has the strongest connections with politics and economics. Shakyamuni, however, did not encourage interest in such worldly things, and so in this regard Buddhism is comparatively weak. In its doctrinal structure and in the way that it relates to society, Buddhism clearly differs from both Christianity and Islam.

6. People Are Equal

Racial discrimination and human rights are problems that always accompany religion. Those fond of power and authority enjoy putting other people in a subordinate position. If you are aware of the history of mankind, however, it is impossible to behave in such an absurd manner. As a member of the Ōtani Branch of the Shin sect, I proposed to the General Manager that we issue a statement declaring our support for human rights and our stand against discrimination. My proposal was met with indifference and half-hearted support. Considering that the Ōtani Branch was founded on a belief in *tariki* (reliance on the power of Amida Buddha) as a means of salvation, it seems to me that it should have a clear statement of purpose that makes its stance clear. Both Luther and Shinran clearly taught people how they should live. Not to take initiatives that would contribute to the betterment of society seems negligent and foolish. Certain Christian groups have taken measure to eliminate discrimination. In comparison, however, Mahayana Buddhism appears to demonstrate little awareness of racial discrimination or human rights abuses. That a religious organization has no statement condemning discrimination and prejudice indicates a lack of awareness on the part of those in positions of power. Such an organization would no doubt strike Luther and Shinran,

おきます。

7. 私自身についての考察

世界三大宗教といわれるものには、人の心を幸せに導くことがらが説かれていますが、人々が教団と教義とを構成していくとき、代表者に特別な意志が生じたときに、宗教の本質とは違う場合があります。

私は、様々な宗教文献を読んで理解する作業が大切なことは理解しています。宗教書はあまりにも多く、まして文化、言語、時代背景の異なる他の宗教文献を読むには、本人にとってその宗教の全体像を理解が出来るように、なれば良いと願います。

全知全能の神、無量光・無量寿の仏、宇宙の創造主等、私たちの持っている尺度では、とても理解できないといえます。神の国、極楽浄土を目の前で証明してくださいと言われると、有限である私たちには不可能です。伝承されている文献を拠りどころとして、各宗教の教学が成り立っていますが、ここで、私自身について考察したいと思います。

各宗教の教義・宗教用語にとらわれないで、本質を理解すべきです。言葉そのものには、現実の実体がともなっていないので、冷静に「言葉の本質」を判断する必要があります。

私は、仏教の浄土真宗の東本願寺教団に属しています。ある友人のプロテスタント牧師と話をしていたとき、「親鸞さんは、阿弥陀仏の直接の救済を説いているのに、親鸞教団に法主・門主・門首とかあるのは、どうしてですか。親鸞さんの教えと矛盾していませんか。」といわれました。「教えと実態が異なる」との指摘は、正に的を得ていると感心しました。日本的な教団形態を説明しても、絶対他力教に立った親鸞からの視点では、「阿弥陀仏の誓願と自分とは直接の確約の関係」であることからして、その間に何人も「仲介者」△として存在することができません。真宗教団成立の歴史からして、「留守式・本願寺住職」等が相応しく思えます。「親鸞の教え」の通りにできるかどうかは、その立場にいる人たちの自覚の問題です。宗教者は、現世に利益を求める、特別な使命がある

neither of whom had any tolerance for human arrogance, as being a collection of clueless idiots. To summarize, I would just like to state that there are some problems regarding the behavior of certain religious leaders.

7. A Look at Myself

The Big Three religions all started out promulgating doctrines that promised to make people happy. As time passed, however, these religions became organized and their teachings became formulated. At the same time, some of their representative leaders were endowed with special powers. The result was something that was at times slightly at odds with the true essence of the religions.

I realize that it is important to undertake the task of reading and understanding various kinds of religious literature. However, there are so many such writings, and those involving different religions require an understanding of many different cultural, linguistic, and historical issues. It is a daunting task. Therefore, I consider myself lucky if I can manage to gain an overall picture of a particular religion.

An omniscient, omnipotent God, a Buddha of infinite light and blessings, the origin of the universe. Given our limitations, it is next to impossible for us to fathom such things, just as it is impossible for us to describe the Kingdom of God or the Paradise of the Pure Land. Looking at the writings that have been handed down and thinking about the teachings of the various religions, I would simply like to say this:

Instead of becoming caught up in details of doctrine and religious terminology, we should strive to understand a religion's essence. Words alone do not reveal reality - it is necessary to find the essence behind the words.

As for me, I belong to the Higashi (East) Hongan-ji Sect of the Jodo Shinshu (True Pure Land) sect of Buddhism. Once I was talking to a friend who is a Protestant pastor, and he asked me, 'Shinran-san preached that salvation comes directly from Amida Buddha. If so, why does a Shinran-affiliated organization need abbots and other such officials? Isn't it a contradiction?' I pointed out that reality and doctrine are different, but at the same time I was impressed by his penetrating remark. I could have explained that it was just the way that a Japanese-style religious

などと言って、人を惑わしていることが多く見られます。先述の図14を見れば、指導的立場の者の都合で、信者の生き方が変わる事があってはならないと思います。心にとめないことが肝要です。

　宗教では、礼拝・修行・修学・鍛錬・作法・伝導・聴聞・黙然・読誦・黙想等が説かれています。それらは、人生の目的でなく、自立を見つめ、知恵を深くするための方法・手立てです。

　教えを盲目的に信じるのでなく、自分で実際に体験すべきです。心静かに真実を求め、真実に生きる正しい歩みが必要です。

organization is structured. However, Shinran's *tariki* doctrine teaches that Amida Buddha's vow to save us establishes a direct covenant between him and us. From that perspective it is true that an Intermediary △ figure should not be necessary. However, having a Shinran-descended abbot and other such aspects are a part of the history of the Shinshu sect, and as such I do not regard them as being inappropriate. Whether or not the people in those positions properly protect Shinran's teaching is another problem. Religious figures sometimes look for worldly profit. They say that they have a special mission and make other such claims that can lead people astray. Looking at the previously mentioned Fig. 14, I feel that believers should not have to change their ways of life to suit the convenience of those in leadership positions. It is important not to be distracted by their claims.

Religions teach the importance of such things as worship, study, discipline, and observance of rules. Training, listening, keeping silent, and reciting are also emphasized. These are not goals in themselves, however, but means to an end that help us acquire self-knowledge and wisdom. Religious teaching should never be accepted blindly; it should be actually experienced first-hand. One should calmly seek the truth and strive to live in a sincere, straightforward manner.

8. 宗教の違いを超えて

　日本仏教では、非常に進化した教学が学べます。キリスト教16世紀のルター以前に13世紀日本仏教の親鸞が、「他力念仏」の教えによる浄土往生の教学を探求しました。そして絶対他力の教学を完成させました。

　さらに、ルターが教学研究以外に、ラテン語聖書しか使わないローマ教会に対して、ドイツ語聖書を使用したことに感心します。現在では、聖書は各国の言葉に翻訳され使用されています。これに対し、日本仏教では、いまだに漢文教典を使用し続けています。これでは、親鸞を宗祖と仰ぐ本願寺教団は、半分の宗教改革状態といえます。親鸞が「ただ信心を要としるべし」、「念仏にまさるべき善なきゆえに」、「他力念仏」を説いているのが大切だからと思えます。しかし、私は格調の高い漢文経典に劣らないような、日本語経典が必要だと思います。これには、日本仏教界全体での取り組みが求められます。後人の活躍に期待します。

8. Transcending Religious Differences

In many of its teachings, Japanese Buddhism was ahead of its time. In the 13th century - three centuries before Luther - Shinran deeply contemplated the existing notion of the *tariki-nenbutsu* as a means of achieving rebirth in the Pure Land and succeeded in bringing the doctrine to completion.

As for Luther, it is impressive that, in addition to his other religious activities, he translated the Bible into German. Until then, the Catholic Church had only used the Latin Bible. Luther translated it into the vernacular, and, since then, the Bible has been translated into almost every language. In comparison, Japanese Buddhism still relies on sutras written in classical Chinese characters. This means that Hongan-ji, which considers Shinran its head, only halfway completed its religious reformation. Shinran's teachings - 'Faith alone is enough,' 'Reciting the *nenbutsu* prayer is all you need to do,' and '*tariki-nenbutsu*' - are of course important. However, I think we also need Japanese-language versions of the sutras that are equal in quality to the classical Chinese renditions. Making this happen will require the cooperative efforts of the entire Japanese Buddhist community. I look forward to seeing what future generations will accomplish.

まとめ

　私は青年期に、キリスト教徒の中で5年間生活するご縁を頂きました。知人の牧師と一緒に、ニュージャージーの聖書研究会に参加させて頂きました。「宗教音楽会」にも招待され、いろいろな宗教、教会の人たちの中で、「正信偈」の一部を調声したこともありました。毎日の祈りを欠かさない、真面目なイスラム教徒のルームメイトと生活したこともあります。他宗教の人たちとの共同生活は、意外に快適でした。

　恩師、元神学校学長デ・ジョーン師と私は、キリスト教と仏教の教義について、何度も話し合いました。キリスト教徒の中に、心の広い温かみを感じる方に出会えた事を、今でも感謝しています。この師の下で、比較宗教学が出来る環境が整いました。二宗教間を往来しての研究は、私には夢のような楽しい時間でした。この続編となる「宗教の羅針盤」は、比較宗教学に類します。

ドルー大学トンプソン学長から卒業証書を授かる (1980)
Receiving diploma from Bard Thompson, Dean of Drew University Graduate School, 1980.

Summary

When I was young, I had the good fortune to live among Christians for five years. Together with a pastor friend, I participated in a Bible study group in New Jersey. I also accepted an invitation to join a religious music society. Surrounded by people of various religious persuasions, I even chanted a part of Shinran's *Shōshinge* (*The Hymn of True Faith*). I had a Muslim roommate who faithfully observed his daily prayers. I found living with people of different faiths to be surprisingly easy.

My teacher, Dr. De Jong, head of the School of Theology, and I had many discussions about Christian and Buddhist doctrines. I am eternally grateful that I was able to meet such a broad-minded, warm-hearted person. Under his guidance, I experienced the perfect environment for the study of comparative religion. To me it was like a dream to be able to go back and forth between religions and compare them. Writing this 'Religion Compass' has been like a continuation of my comparative religion studies.

デ・ジョーン夫妻と (1979)
With Dr. and Mrs. De Jong, 1979.

友人たちとリバティーパークで (1978)
With friends in Liberty State Park, NJ, 1978.

比較宗教学について、述べてみましょう。比較宗教学を武術で喩えれば、東西混合武術のようなものです。西洋のフェンシングでなく、日本の剣道でもありません。武術を体得する人によって、その人の立つ位置と方法論が異なります。もし、自分の属する武術が一番と主張したり、断言したりすると、他の武術の人たちはそれを受け入れず、認めることはないでしょう。しかし、東西混合武術は両方の武術を体得し、自由に体現します。

それは、一般に宗教学でやっているような、各宗教の歴史的な経緯を記したり、教義を要約したり、地図上に羅列したりするようなものでもありません。

比較研究に取り組むには、「平行視点」を持つ必要があります。研究対象となる課題に対し、考察範囲と分析システムを確立させる必要があります。研究テーマが定まっても、その研究対象の宗教、思想は、異なった時代、文化、民族の中で成立してきたものです。従って、思想間の優劣の証明を目的とするものではありません。論述時は、どこまでも平行視線で、冷静に、的確に課題を論じます。それは同時に、自己の帰属する宗教に対しての執着心と向き合うことが求められます。自分の居る場所は、せいぜい最後に私見を述べる時ぐらいです。比較宗教学は、時代・文化・言語・国家・民族に影響されない学問分野ですが、課題とする宗教の数だけ、基礎知識習得のため時間が必要となります。

私は本願寺派の青木寛誠氏と共に、平成8・9年に「東西合同蓮如上人500回遠忌記念催し会」を考案しました。権力者豊臣秀吉と徳川家康によって、本願寺は東西に分裂しました。平成7年には多くの仲間が加わり、蓮如上人を偲ぶことで、500年前には一つの本願寺の友であった事を体感できる催しを行いました。俳優松方弘樹さんも参加しました。その後、私たちの心には、秀吉と家康の呪縛は不要と考えるようになりました。

平成21・22年には、再び青木氏と「親鸞さまのお通りイン関西」の催しに取り組みました。私たちは、親鸞聖人750御遠忌法要で親鸞聖人に出会うだけでは満足出来ませんでした。平成の時代に、苦悩を持って生きていた若い親鸞聖人との出会いを体感できる催しを、関西各地の有志

Speaking of comparative religion, if we were to compare it to a martial art, it would neither be Western-style fencing nor Japanese kendo; rather, we would call it a mixed martial art. Every martial art has its own methodology, and every person who has mastered a martial art will follow that martial art's principles. However, if you claim that the martial art that you practice is the best, practitioners of other martial arts will not accept what you say. A mixed martial art, however, combines methodologies and freely embodies them.

The study of comparative religion does not involve, as is normally the case with the study of a religion, relating that religion's historical details, summarizing its doctrine, or showing where it exists on a map.

The field of comparative religion requires looking at religions with a 'parallel viewpoint'. In order to research the study topic, it is necessary set the scope of the examination and to establish an analytic system. Even though the research topic has been decided, it must be remembered that the religion and the religious thought to be studied came about in a different historical period, in a different culture, and in a different ethnic setting. The intent of the study is not to prove the superiority of one religion over another. When we engage in discussion, we approach the topic calmly and accurately, maintaining a 'parallel viewpoint'. At the same time, we must come to terms with our feelings of attachment to our own religion. At the very least, we should keep any personal opinions until the very end. An academic field, comparative religion is not influenced by historical, cultural, linguistic, national, or ethnic considerations. However, it takes time to acquire basic knowledge about the religions to be studied.

From 1996 to 1997, Kanjō Aoki, the abbot of a West Hongan-ji affiliated temple, and I organized a joint East/West Hongan-ji commemoration of the 500th anniversary of Rennyo's death. Hongan-ji, a Shinshu-sect temple headed by Shinran's descendant, Rennyo, had been split into two temples - East Hongan-ji and West Hongan-ji - by warlords Hideyoshi Toyotomi and Ieyasu Tokugawa. In 1995, I had gotten together with many of my associates to pay remembrance to Rennyo. At that time, we were able to experience what it must have felt like when Hongan-ji had been one entity 500 years ago. This encouraged us to organize the joint commemoration. Famous actor Hiroki Matsukata also joined in this event. After it, we all came away

寺院の参加を頂いて行いました。光永覚道大阿闍梨と桂花團治さんが参加しました。

　私のドルー時代を回想すると、部屋の中央に２枚の大きなドアの机があり、その上に英訳と和訳の新旧約聖書、漢文と和訳と一部英訳の仏教聖典、課題対象となる聖人達の著書や関連書籍、それに言語の異なる宗教用語の解説書、さらに数種類の英日・日英の翻訳辞書等を置いていました。さらに、論文にする場合は、引用文献の表記、重要単語の説明作業まで必要になります。

仏跡参拝（インド）(2015)
Worshipping at an Indian Buddhist site, 2015.

　マザーテレサが、「私は、無視されると悲しい」といわれたことがあります。人権を無視するような、宗教者としての資質に欠ける人は対象外となります。真面目に人の心と向かい合うことがないと、他宗教の人たちとは交流が成立しません。現代は、私たちが思っているより世界の人達が身近になり、世界中の様々な価値観が入り乱れています。インターネットで、時代は一変しました。現在人は、インターネットによって国境を感じない生き方を身につけました。そこで、自分の生き方を理解する為に、宗教における「羅針盤」が必要と考えるようになりました。友人がこの本に対し、「宗教の垣根を越えての考えに、時代が追いついてきましたね」と言われました。私は、どの宗教に帰属していても、「宗教の本質から目を離さない生き方を願う」人たちと、知り合うことに喜びを感じます。

　「縁」とは、不思議なものです。40年ほど前に龍谷大学で、仏教の「宿業」とキリスト教の「宿命」というテーマの、パネルデスカッションがありました。２人の宗教学者が「宿業」と「宿命」について説明し、宗教観の違いを見いだすことで時間が過ぎました。結果については、参加者の判断に委ねて終わりました。私には、とても楽しくて有意義な時間でし

feeling that the spell that Hideyoshi and Ieyasu had cast on Hongan-ji had been broken.

From 2009 to 2010, I again collaborated with Abbot Aoki and helped organize an event called 'Shinran-sama no Otōri in Kansai' ('Roads Traveled by Shinran in the Kansai District'). Our motivation in doing so was that we felt that something extra was needed to complement Shinran's 750th memorial celebration. We wanted to introduce people to the young struggling Shinran who managed to overcome many obstacles. Thanks to the participation of temples from every part of Kansai, we were able to do this by retracing some of the young Shinran's footsteps. Kakuto Mitsunaga, a *dai-ajari* - a Living Buddha who has completed the *sennichi kaihōgyō*, an arduous seven-year ascetic training regimen - and traditional storyteller Hanadanji Katsura also took part in the event.

親鸞様のお通りイン関西(2009)
Taking part in the 'Shinran-sama no Otōri in Kansai' event, 2009.

When I recall my time at Drew University, I remember that there were two big doors that served as desks in the middle of my room. On them were English and Japanese versions of the New Testament, as well as Chinese, Japanese, and some English versions of Buddhist scriptures. There were also writings of saints and holy men and related works. There were also commentaries on different linguistic renderings of religious terminology and several English-Japanese, Japanese-English dictionaries. And when I was writing my thesis, there were footnote compilations, as well as explanations of important vocabulary.

Mother Theresa once said, 'It makes me sad when I'm ignored.' Indeed, Religious figures who would ignore her and ignore human rights do not merit consideration. If we cannot look sincerely into the hearts of others, then we cannot relate to people of different faiths. At present, the people of the world are living in closer proximity than ever before, and the values of

た。その後、「これでは、終わらせられない」と考えるようになりました。

若者は最上への挑戦権をもっています。自分の人生を創出することができるのは、素晴らしいですね。私は命ある限り、比較宗教学へ探究心を持ち続け、「行って、見て、聞いて、考えて、実行」する生き方で励みたいと考えています。

私には後人に、是非挑戦して欲しいテーマが2つあります。

恩師のカソリックのコレス牧師との楽しい時間を回想します。トーマス・アクイムスが著した「神学大全」に書かれてある「神の意志」の概念と、親鸞の著した「教行信証」にある「証」の概念が、類似している事を熱く語り合いました。宗教、時代、を越えた真実の探求者達の対話は、私たちを導く「羅針盤」になります。

ダンテの「神曲」にある地獄と源信の「往生要集」の地獄の比較研究。それに対して、ユダヤ教・キリスト教・イスラム教の説く「神の国」と仏教の説く「極楽・浄土」の比較研究。この研究は、自分の宗教に対する心を豊かにします。時間を要するのは必然ですが、宗教の本質を知る方向に向かう事になっていくでしょう。

これらは、40年前からの私の研究課題でもあります。世界の宗教巨人それぞれには、自分の属している宗教の開祖の説く教えの縛りがあります。開祖の説く教理に従順な巨人もいれば、開祖にはない発想を持って語る巨人もいます。同じ宗教であっても、巨人たちは新しい思想を展開しています。巨人達の生き方を知ることは、大変楽しい作業です。多くの巨人たちのことを、知りたいと思いませんか。

ある時、机の上を眺めていて、心静かに目を閉じると、キリスト教の「エラスムスとルター」、仏教の「親鸞と道元」、彼らが楽しそうに自由に対話している思惟空間があることを感じました。その空間にいる巨人達を図面の上で描いてみると、感性の強い宗教の巨人たちの声が、近くに聞こえてくるように感じます。

この「宗教の羅針盤」読んで、読者が平行の視線を持ち、時間と空間の束縛を離れて、巨人たちの思想を理解し、自分の立つ位置が理解できれば、「宗教の羅針盤」を使いこなせたといえると思います。

　　　　　　　　　　　　　　　　　　　　　　　　　　西川義光

the world are jumbled together. The Internet has completely changed the world, making the notion of borders meaningless. Because of this, I began to think that it would be good to have a kind of 'religion compass' that would help people find their way in life. As a friend said to me regarding this book, 'The time has come for a way of thinking that overcomes the barriers between religions.' No matter what religion a person belongs to, as long as they strive to live in such a manner that they never lose sight of that religion's true essence, I will be pleased to make their acquaintance.

Fate works in strange ways. Forty years ago I attended a panel discussion at Ryukoku University. The topics under discussion were the Buddhist concept of karma and the Christian notion of predestination. Two scholars of religion explained these concepts, and, as time passed, the different points of view of the two religions were revealed. It was left up to the participants to draw their own conclusions. For me it was a very enjoyable and meaningful time, and later I thought, 'I don't want it to end there.'

Young people have the right to set their sights high and challenge the summits. Carving out the course of your own life is a wonderful thing. As long as I am alive, I want to continue to pursue my interest in comparative religion. 'Go, look, listen, think, act!' is how I want to live.

There are two things that I would encourage future generations to think about:

1) I recall the pleasant time spent in the company of my teacher, Father Cores. We enthusiastically discussed the similarity between the concept of God's will put forth in Thomas Aquinas' *Summa Theologiae* and that of the concept of proof set forth in Shinran's *Kyōgyōshinshō*. When people transcend religion and historical era in the search for truth, their dialog becomes like a compass that shows the way forward.

2) Compare hell as depicted in Dante's *The Divine Comedy* with hell as depicted in Genshin's *Ōjōyōshū* (*The Essentials of Rebirth in the Pure Land*). After that, compare the Kingdom of God of Judaism, Christianity, and Islam with Buddhism's Pure Land Paradise. Doing so will enrich your view of your own religion. It will no doubt take time, but it will set you on the path to understanding the essence of your religion.

For the last forty years these have been my research themes. Every

参考文献

聖書（旧約聖書・新約聖書）

仏教経典

コーラン

真宗聖教全書

デジデリウス・エラスムス『自由意志論』

マルティン・ルター『奴隷意志論』

親鸞『教行信証』

道元『正法眼蔵』

西川義光 "Power of Self and the Other Power in Christianity and Buddhism."
（米国ドルー大学学位論文 1980）

great religious personage has ties to the founder of the religion to which he belongs. Some of these religious giants adhere faithfully to the founder's principles, while others put forth new ideas. Religions develop and progress thanks to these giants. Learning how these giants lived is very enjoyable. Wouldn't you like to know about their lives?

Once, when looking at the surface of my desk, I closed by eyes in contemplation. The Christians, Erasmus and Luther, and the Buddhists, Shinran and Dōgen, seemed to inhabit a common space and be engaged in a free-wheeling, convivial conversation. As I made graphic representations of their doctrines, I seemed to be able to feel the vibrations given off by these giants.

If the reader who reads this 'Religion Compass' maintains a 'parallel viewpoint', detaches himself or herself from the bonds of space and time, and understands the ideas of the giants, then he or she can find his or her place in the universe. He or she will have mastered the use of the 'religion compass'.

Gikō Nishikawa

References

The Bible (Old Testament, New Testament)

Buddhist Sutras

The Koran

Shinshū Shōgyō Zensho (Shinshū-sect Buddhist Sermons)

De Libero Arbitrio Diatribe Sive Collatio (On Free Will), Desiderius Erasmus

De Servo Arbitrio (On the Bondage of the Will), Martin Luther

Kyōgyō shinshō (The True Teaching, Practice, faith, and Realization of the Pure Land Way), Shinran

Shōbōgenzō (Treasury of the True Dharma Eye), Dōgen

'Power of Self and the Other Power in Christianity and Buddhism', Gikō Nishikawa (Drew University M.A. thesis. May, 1980.)

◆ 著者紹介

西川 義光（にしかわ ぎこう）

略　　歴

昭和25年　滋賀県生
昭和44年　京都 大谷高等学校卒業
昭和47年　龍谷大学(真宗学専攻)学士 卒業
昭和50年　ニューヨーク日本語教室 講師
昭和51年　ニューヨーク市立大学 哲学 履修
昭和55年　ドルー大学院 キリスト教学専攻
　　　　　MA 卒業
昭和56年　大阪 上宮高校非常勤講師
昭和62年　社会福祉法人　一向山福祉会理事長
平成08年　真宗 専称寺住職
平成17年　比叡山坂本保育園長
平成18年　専称寺保育園長
○　ニューヨーク仏教会の関 法善に師事

専称寺
　〒520-0113　滋賀県大津市坂本8丁目31-25

しゅうきょうのらしんばん
宗教の羅針盤
ズバリ!! 図式で考える

発 行 日　————　2018年8月15日　初版第1刷
著　　者　————　西川 義光
発 行 者　————　宮内 久

海青社
Kaiseisha Press
　〒520-0112　大津市日吉台2丁目16-4
Tel. (077) 577-2677　Fax (077) 577-2688
http://www.kaiseisha-press.ne.jp
郵便振替　01090-1-17991

● 定価はカバーに表示してあります。落丁乱丁はお取り替えいたします。
● © 2018　Printed in Japan　ISBN978-4-86099-337-5 C0014

◆ Author

Gikō Nishikawa

Personal History

1950: Born in Shiga Prefecture, Japan.
1969: Graduated from Ōtani High School, Kyoto, Japan.
1972: Received B.A. in Shin Sect Buddhism, Ryukoku University, Japan.
1976: Studied philosophy at New York City University, USA.
1980: Received M.A. in Christian theology from Drew University, NJ, USA.
1981: Taught at Uenomiya High School, Osaka, Japan.
1987 to present: Director, Ikkozan Welfare Association, Social Welfare Corporation.
1995 to present: Head abbot of Senshō-ji Temple, Otsu City, Shiga Prefecture, Japan.
2005 to present: Principal of Hieizan-Sakamoto Nursery School.
2006 to present: Principal of Senshō-ji Nursery School.
Studied under Rev. Hōzen Seki of The New York Buddhist Church.

Senshō-ji Temple
　3-31-25 Sakamoto, Ōtsu City, Shiga Prefecture, 520-0113, Japan

---

The Religion Compass
A Graphic Approach to Understanding Religions

Gikō Nishikawa
©2018

First published Aug. 2018
ISBN978-4-86099-337-5 C0014
Printed in Japan

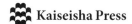

Kaiseisha Press

2-16-4 Hiyoshidai, Ōtsu City, Shiga Prefecture, 520-0112, Japan
http://www.kaiseisha-press.ne.jp/

◆ 海青社の本・好評発売中 ◆

創作ORIGAMI叢書1 香鈴（かりん）
松井佳容子 著

「花あり、箱あり、飛行機あり」とバラエティーにとんだ作品が紹介されています。ビギナーからベテランまで楽しめる創作ORIGAMIです。読者は折りながら、知らず知らずのうちに、その豊かな遊び心や造形感覚を発見することでしょう。
〔ISBN978-4-86099-327-6/A4判/34頁/本体1,241円〕

白洲正子と歩く琵琶湖　江南編・カミと仏が融けあう処
大沼芳幸 著

随筆家 白洲正子は近江を愛し紀行文の多くに題材としてとりあげた。ビギナー正子は近江の文化遺産を"白洲正子の視線"からたどる。江南編では、湖西・湖南・湖東地方を対象に、自然に宿るカミの姿と、カミと仏が融合する聖地を巡る。
〔ISBN978-4-86099-333-7/四六判/158頁/本体1,700円〕

琵琶湖八珍　湖魚の宴絶品メニュー
大沼芳幸 著

琵琶湖八珍の多種多彩なメニューレシピをオールカラーで270余掲載。さらにギル・バスを含む外来種四種を裏八珍として掲載。美しい琵琶湖に思いを馳せ、美味しい琵琶湖八珍を提言する。
〔ISBN978-4-86099-309-2/A5判/196頁/本体1,833円〕

環境を守る森をしらべる
原田 洋・鈴木伸一 ほか3名著

都市部や工場などに人工的に造成された環境保全林が、地域本来の植生状態にどれくらい近づいたかを調べて評価する方法を紹介。環境保全林の作り方を述べた小社刊「環境を守る森をつくる」の続刊。
〔ISBN978-4-86099-338-2/四六判/158頁/本体1,600円〕

環境を守る森をつくる
原田 洋・矢ケ崎朋樹 著

環境保全林は「ふるさとの森」や「いのちの森」とも呼ばれ、生物多様性や自然性など、土地本来の生物的環境を守る機能を併せ持つ。本書ではそのつくり方から働きまでを、著者の研究・活動の経験をもとに解説。
〔ISBN978-4-86099-324-5/四六判/158頁/本体1,600円〕

国 宝 建 築 探 訪
中野達夫 著

岩手の中尊寺金色堂から長崎の大浦天主堂まで、全国125カ所、209件の国宝建築を木材研究者の立場から語る探訪記。制作年から構造、建築素材、専門用語も解説。木を愛し木を知り尽くした人ならではのユニークなコメントも楽しめる。
〔ISBN978-4-906165-82-7/A5判/310頁/本体2,800円〕

近世庶民の日常食　百姓は米を食べられなかったか
有薗正一郎 著

近世に生きた我々の先祖たちは、住む土地で穫れる食材群をうまく組み合わせて食べる「地産地消」の賢い暮らしをしていた。近世の史資料からごく普通の人々の日常食を考証し、各地域の持つ固有の性格を明らかにする。
〔ISBN978-4-86099-231-6/A5判/219頁/本体1,800円〕

ク リ と 日 本 文 明
元木 靖 著

生命の木「クリ」と日本文明との関わりを、古代から現代までの歴史のながれに視野を広げて解き明かす。クリに関する研究をベースに文明史の観点と地理学的な研究方法を組み合わせて、日本の文明史の特色に迫る。
〔ISBN978-4-86099-301-6/A5判/242頁/本体3,500円〕

読みたくなる「地図」西日本編　日本の都市はどう変わったか
平岡昭利 編

明治期と現代の地形図の比較から都市の変貌を読み解く。本書では近畿地方から沖縄まで43都市を対象に、地域に関わりの深い研究者が解説。「考える地理」の書物として好適。地図の拡大表示が便利なPDF版も発売中。
〔ISBN978-4-86099-314-6/B5判/127頁/本体1,600円〕

読みたくなる「地図」東日本編　日本の都市はどう変わったか
平岡昭利 編

明治期と現代の地形図の比較から都市の変貌を読み解く。北海道から北陸地方まで49都市を対象に、その地に関わりの深い研究者が解説。「考える地理」の基本的な書物として好適。地図の拡大表示が便利なPDF版も発売中。
〔ISBN978-4-86099-313-9/B5判/133頁/本体1,600円〕

旧約聖書を推理する　本当は誰が書いたか
フリードマン,R.E. 著・松本英昭 訳

古来さまざまな神学上の問題を提起してきたエデンの園のエピソードは、実は、二つの全く異なる文書を合成したものだった。旧約聖書の「数奇な生い立ち」を、苛烈な古代近東の政治風土と重ね合わせながら推理する。
〔ISBN978-4-906165-28-5/A5判/354頁/本体2,621円〕

＊表示価格は本体価格（税別）です。